TODD KARR'S
Backyard Magic

Be a magician! Use things you find in your own backyard!

Illustrated by Ellen Blonder

SCHOLASTIC INC.

Cartwheel BOOKS®

New York   Toronto   London   Auckland   Sydney

For
Jovann, Alexander, and Schuyler—
my magic boys.
—T. K.

Cover photograph by Beth Phillips.

ISBN 0-590-40021-5

Text copyright © 1996 by Todd Karr.
Illustrations copyright © 1996 by Ellen Blonder.
All rights reserved. Published by Scholastic Inc.
CARTWHEEL BOOKS and the CARTWHEEL BOOKS logo are registered trademarks of Scholastic Inc.

12 11 10 9 8 7 6 5 4 3 2 1   6 7 8 9/9 0 1/0

Printed in the U.S.A.   08

First Scholastic printing, April 1996

Contents

Welcome!

I think the world would be a lot nicer if there were more magicians. How beautiful it would be to have magic everywhere!

That's why I wrote this book. I want to give this magic to you so you can fill the world with wonder!

I believe that nature is full of magic, too. So all of the magic in this book happens outdoors. You can become better friends with nature as you do your magic!

And do you know what? You're full of magic, too! So believe you're a real magician and have fun creating the magic in this book.

—Todd Karr

About Todd Karr

Todd Karr has been a magician for over 20 years. He performs his magic throughout the United States and Europe. He has created magic in theaters and on television and for princes and princesses. Wherever he performs, he dazzles people with his magic! Now he brings his magic to you—in his first book for children.

Make Your Magic Work

Before you do your magic for your friends, try it out at home—by yourself—in front of a mirror. Practice what you are going to say, too.

Believe that what you're doing is *real* magic.

Always have your friend stand in front of you so he or she won't see anything that should be a secret.

Always put your magician's tools in a safe place, like a backpack, so your friend won't find out your secrets.

Never tell how you did your magic. If your friend asks, you can say, "It's magic!" or "It's a secret!" If your friend tells you how he or she thinks you did it, just smile!

Never do the same magic twice for the same person because he or she will be looking more closely the second time.

Earth Word

Make magic writing appear on your arm!

Your magician's tools: a thin bar of soap and a cup of water.

1. Decide on a word that is no more than four or five letters long. It can be your friend's name or nickname, a club password, a secret magic word, or even a symbol like a lightning bolt.

2. Roll up your sleeves.

3. Dip a corner of the soap in the cup of water.

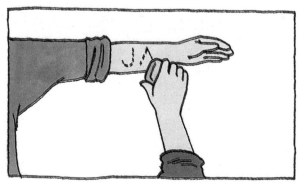

4. Using the soap like a pencil, write the word on your arm in big, capital letters. Dip the soap in the water for each letter. Be neat!

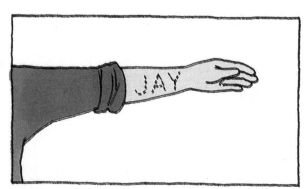

5. When you have finished, keep your sleeve rolled up so the word doesn't get messy. **Now your friend can come see your magic!**

6. Using a stick or your finger, write the word in the dirt in front of you.

7. Repeat the magic words, "Earth, Earth, speak our word" with your friend. Rub the dirt around to erase your word.

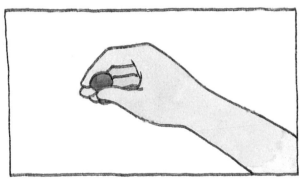

8. Pick up some of the dirt.

9. Rub the dirt back and forth on your arm where you wrote the letters with the soap.

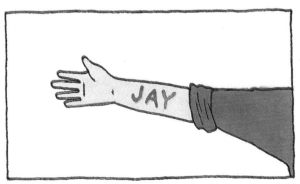

10. The dirt should stick to the soap letters on your arm. It looks like the earth has written a word on your skin!

11. Some kinds of dirt stick better than others. Make sure you try out the dirt on your *other* arm before doing this magic for your friend.

Money from Nowhere

Make a coin appear inside a folded leaf!

Your magician's tools: two coins exactly alike and a roll of double-sided tape.

1. Put one of the coins in your pocket. Stick a small piece of tape onto the back of the other coin.

2. Find a leaf. Stick the coin onto the back of the leaf.

3. Carefully place the leaf on the ground, with the coin facing down.
Now your friend can come see your magic!

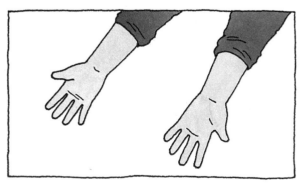

4. Roll up your sleeves and show that your hands are empty.

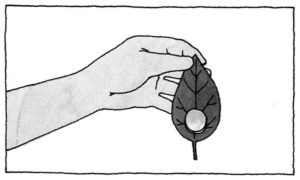

5. Pick up the leaf as if it were a regular leaf. Hold it by the top point with the coin at the back.

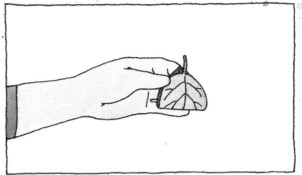

6. Fold the leaf in half so the coin is inside.

7. Hold the leaf folded in half.

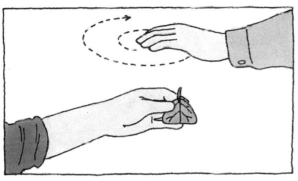

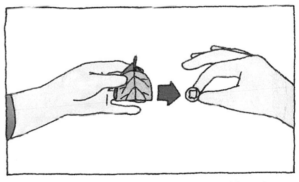

8. Ask your friend to wave her or his hand over the leaf and to say the magic words, "Metal of the earth, come here now."

9. Reach inside and pull out the coin. Show it to your friend with the tape side facing you.

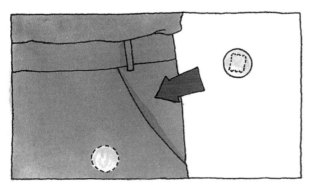

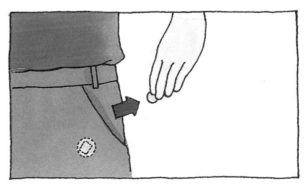

10. Put the coin in your pocket. Set the leaf down.

11. If your friend wants to see the coin, reach into your pocket and take out the coin that does not have any tape on it. Let your friend see it.

The Floating Branch

Make a twig rise into the air!

Your magician's tools: a spool of black thread and a pair of scissors. (Try to wear dark pants and a dark shirt for this magic.)

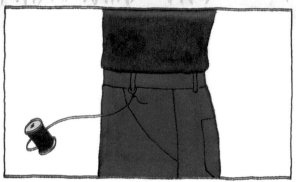

1. Tie one end of the thread to the belt loop on the left side of your pants.

2. Cut the thread a little shorter than the length of your outstretched arm.

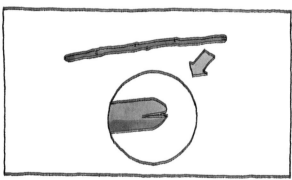

3. Find a small branch. Use your fingers or your scissors to make a crack in the end of the branch.

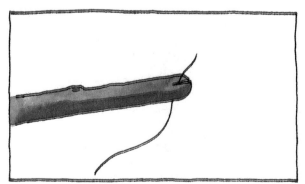

4. Slip the end of the thread into the crack.

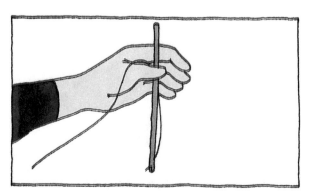

5. Hold the top of the stick in your left hand. The cracked end is at the bottom. The thread goes over your thumb. Hold the branch loosely.

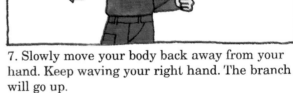

6. **Now your friend can come see your magic!**
Hold the hand with the stick in front of your belly
button. Wave your right hand mysteriously over
the branch.

7. Slowly move your body back away from your
hand. Keep waving your right hand. The branch
will go up.

8. Wave your right hand again. This time, slowly
move your body forward—toward the branch.
The branch will go down.

9. Take the branch with your right hand.

10. Hand the branch to your friend. As you do,
the thread gets pulled out of the crack.

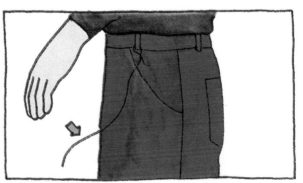

11. The thread falls to your side, where your
friend will not notice it. If you are wearing dark
pants, the thread will be even more hidden.

Seeing the Future

Know what your friend will choose!

Your magician's tools: a thin black marker, a small paper bag, a piece of paper, a smooth stick, a leaf, a stone, and a flower.

1. Use the marker to write YOU WILL CHOOSE THE STONE on the piece of paper. Put the paper in the bag.

2. Write YOU WILL CHOOSE THE LEAF on the leaf. Put the leaf in the bag.

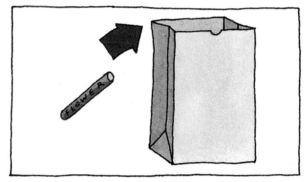

3. Carefully write FLOWER on the stick in small letters. Put the stick in the bag.

4. Put the stone and the flower in the bag. **Now your friend can come see your magic!**

5. Take the leaf, stone, and flower out of the bag and set them in front of your friend. Put the leaf on the ground with the writing side down so she won't see it.

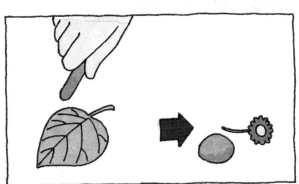

6. Hand your friend the stick and say, "Point to one of these things. But I already know which one you will choose!"

7. When your friend has pointed to one, push aside the other two objects.

8. IF SHE CHOSE THE LEAF, ask her to turn it over. She will read, "YOU WILL CHOOSE THE LEAF." Then turn over the other objects to show that nothing is written on them.

9. IF SHE CHOSE THE FLOWER, tell her, "On the stick, I wrote down which thing you would choose. Look." She will see the word "FLOWER" on the stick.

10. IF SHE CHOSE THE STONE, have her look in the bag. She will find the paper that says, "YOU WILL CHOOSE THE STONE."

11. Put everything back in the bag. Remember, of course, that you can never do this in front of the same friend twice!

Amazing Pinecones

Make a pinecone appear out of thin air!

Your magician's tools: a spool of black thread, a pair of scissors, a small paper bag, a pinecone, and a cloth napkin or handkerchief that is dark or patterned.

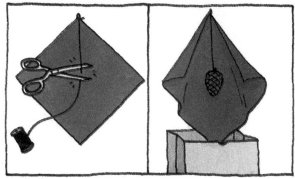

1. Tie the end of the thread to a corner of the napkin. Unwind the thread to reach the center of the napkin. Cut the thread. Tie the pinecone to the end of the thread. Put the napkin in the bag.

Now your friend can come see your magic!
2. Take the napkin out of the bag by holding the tied corner. The pinecone should hang inside the napkin so your friend can't see it.

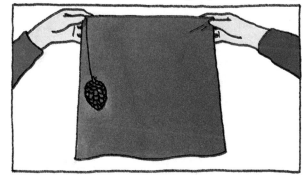

3. Hold another corner of the napkin with your other hand. The pinecone should hang behind the napkin. Gently shake the napkin to show it is empty.

4. Gather up the corners of the napkin in your hand to form a bag.

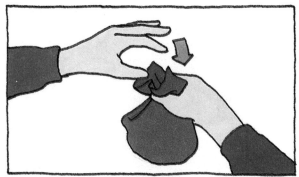

5. Say to your friend, "There's an invisible pine tree here. I'll pick a pinecone from it." Pretend to pick a pinecone and place it in the napkin.

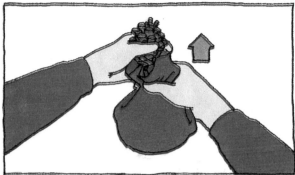

6. Reach into the napkin and pull out the pinecone to show your friend. Keep the thread hidden behind your hand.

7. Put the pinecone back in the napkin.

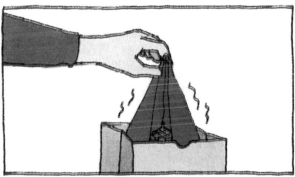

8. Hold the napkin over the paper bag. Let go of all the corners except the top corner that is tied with the thread. Shake the napkin as if you were dropping the pinecone into the bag.

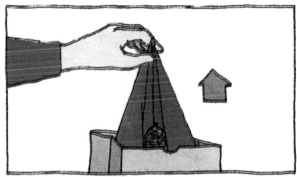

9. Lift the napkin out of the bag. The pinecone should stay hidden inside the napkin.

10. Say, "We're done making pinecones appear." Put the napkin away someplace, such as your backpack.

11. Your friend will think there is a pinecone in the bag. Say, "Pinecone, vanish!" Turn the bag so your friend can look inside and see that it is empty!

Suncatcher

Change sunlight into yellow flowers!

Your magician's tools: two envelopes, a roll of double-sided tape, and a pair of scissors.

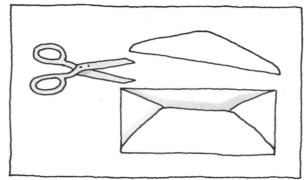

1. Cut off the flap of one of the envelopes.

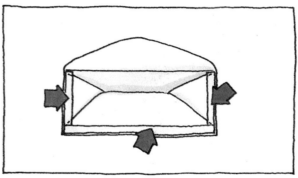

2. On the back of the other envelope, stick double-sided tape on the two sides and the bottom.

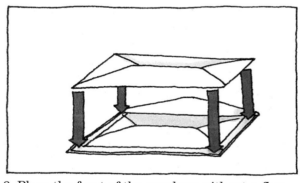

3. Place the front of the envelope without a flap onto the tape. Line up the edges carefully. This makes a double envelope with two sections.

4. Find some dandelions or other small yellow flowers. Break off the stems. Place the buds in the back section of the double envelope.
Now your friend can come see your magic!

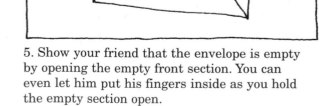

5. Show your friend that the envelope is empty by opening the empty front section. You can even let him put his fingers inside as you hold the empty section open.

6. Say that you are going to catch sunshine in the envelope. Hold the empty section of the envelope open underneath the sunlight. If it's not sunny, just hold it up to the sky.

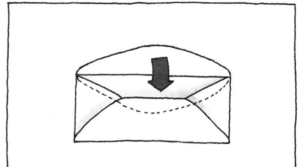

7. Ask your friend to tell you when he thinks you have caught enough sunshine. When he says you have enough, close the flap.

8. Say, "We've got some yellow sunshine in the envelope. Let's turn it into something yellow we can touch." Have your friend say with you the magic words, "Sunlight, bright light."

9. Have your friend hold out his hands and cup them together.

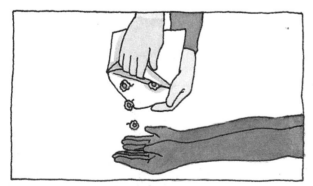

10. Turn the envelope upside down over his hands. Open the back section so the flowers can fall into his hands.

11. Your friend can keep the flowers. Put the envelope in your backpack. If your friend asks to see it, say, "Only the magician can touch it!"

More Changes!

By using the double envelope from "Suncatcher," you can change many things into other things! Just put something, like a flower, into the back section.

Show the empty front section. Put in anything you'd like, such as petals. Close the envelope, then open it, and pull out the flower.

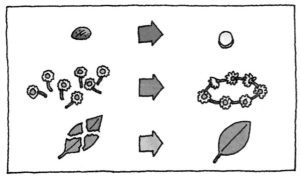

In the same way, you can change a small stone into a coin, daisies into a daisy chain, a torn leaf into a whole one . . .

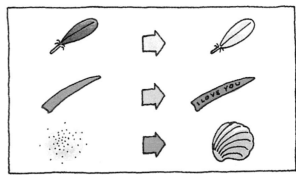

. . . a black feather into a white feather, a blade of grass into a blade of grass with a message written on it, or sand into a seashell.

You can also make almost anything appear! Place anything small, like a piece of bark, into the back section.

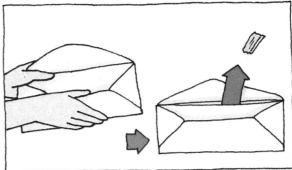

Show that the empty part has nothing in it. Close the envelope and say some magic words. Then open the back section to show what has appeared!

Water from a Stone

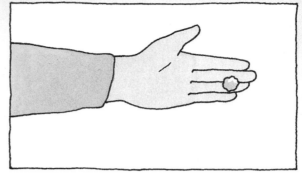

Ask your friend to hand you a stone. You squeeze it tightly and water drips from it!

Your secret: Clipped between your fingers is a small cotton ball soaked with water. Press this against the stone as you squeeze.

Magnetic Weed

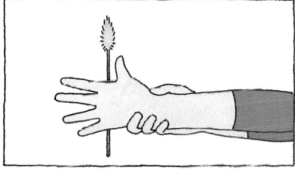

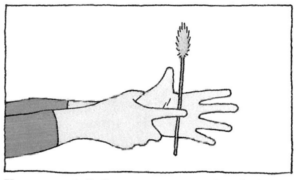

Pull a long weed out of the ground. Hold it in your hand. Grip your arm with the other hand to steady it. Open your hand. The weed sticks to your hand!

Your secret: Before you open your hand, slide your index finger in to hold the weed in place.

Moon Mirror

Hold a small mirror under the moon. Now breathe on the mirror so the glass fogs up. A picture of the moon appears!

Your secret: Before you begin, draw a moon on the mirror with chalk. Next, lightly wipe the chalk off the mirror with a soft cloth. When you breathe on the mirror, the moon will appear.

Growing by Magic

Make a plant grow by magic!

Your magician's tools: a seed, such as an acorn or a watermelon seed, or something that looks like a seed, such as a pebble, a nut, or a berry.

1. Find a small plant (about eight inches high) growing in dirt but not in grass.

2. Next to the plant, dig a shallow hole long enough for the plant to lie in. To dig, use your hands, a stick, or a shovel.

3. Carefully bend the plant so it lies in the hole. If you think the plant will break, stop and choose a thicker plant.

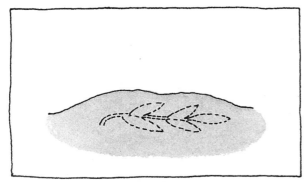

4. Cover the plant with dirt so that the plant is completely hidden.
Now your friend can come see your magic!

5. Show your friend the seed. With your finger, push it into the ground next to the plant.

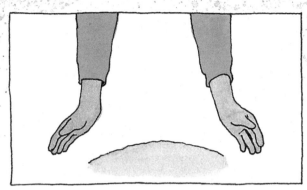

6. Chant "Abracadabra!" over and over with your friend. As you do, kneel and place your hands on the ground to the left and right of the plant.

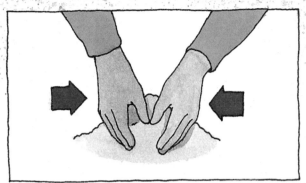

7. Bring your hands together, sliding the dirt and the hidden plant with them. The plant ends up bunched between your hands.

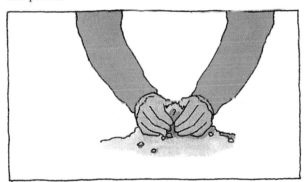

8. As you and your friend keep saying the magic word, gently rub your hands together. The dirt will fall out of your hands.

9. Open your hands and show the plant.

10. If the plant does not spring back up, gently pull it up straight.

11. Leave the plant where it is! Nature will keep it growing!

Invisible Rain

Make rain appear in a cup!

Your magician's tools: two paper cups, a paper bag, and a pair of scissors. Cut off the bottom of one cup. Cut the rim off the other cup.

1. Put the cup with no bottom into the cup with no rim. Fill them halfway with water. Put the cups into the bag. Carefully set the bag on the ground.

Now your friend can come see your magic!
2. Take the cups out of the bag. Hold the cups near the top so your friend can't see the cut one. Do not let your friend see the water inside.

3. Show your friend that the bag is empty.

4. Set the bag on the ground and put the cups back in the bag.

5. Take out the cup with no bottom. Place the cup into your other hand and hold it by the bottom so your friend can't see the hole!

6. Turn the cup upside down to show it is empty. A few drops of water may drip out. Just say, "I was trying to catch rain in this cup this morning. I only caught a few drops."

7. Carefully put the cup back in the bag, inside the other cup.

8. Raise your hands in the air and ask the clouds, "Will you send us rain?"

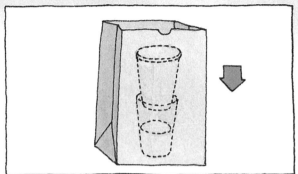

9. Take out the cups.

10. Pour the water on the ground.

11. Put the cups back in the bag, and put the bag in a safe place like your backpack.

The Mystic Triangle

Make a mysterious mark appear on your friend's hand!

Your magician's tools: a sugar cube and a pencil. Find a stick and place it on the ground near you.

1. Using the pencil, draw a triangle on the sugar cube. Trace over the lines a few times to make them dark.

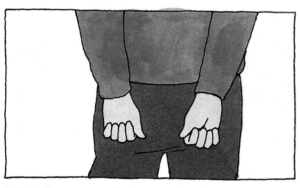

2. Put the sugar cube in your hand. Place both hands behind your back.
Now your friend can come see your magic!

3. With your hands still behind your back, tell your friend, "You're going to do some magic today." Ask her to pick up the stick.

4. Turn around and put your hands in front of you.

5. Lick the thumb of your empty hand. Press that thumb onto the triangle on the sugar cube. When you lift up your thumb, there will be a copy of the triangle on your thumb.

6. Ask your friend to draw an invisible triangle in the air using the stick.

7. Turn back around. Put your hands behind your back. Tell your friend to hold out her empty hand flat with her palm toward the ground.

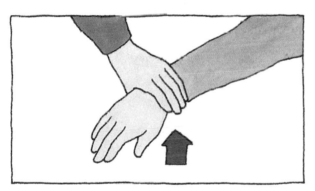

8. Say, "It has to be higher." Grasp her hand with your fingers on top and your thumb pressing on her palm. This puts a copy of the triangle onto her palm. Move her hand up a few inches.

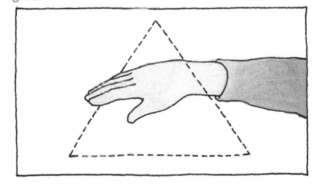

9. Ask her to keep her hand open, palm down, and to make another invisible triangle in the air. Then ask her to put her hand into the center of the invisible triangle.

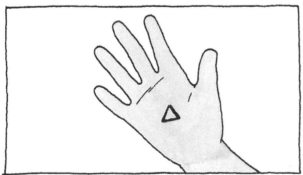

10. Tell her to turn over her hand. She will be surprised to see a triangle on her palm.

11. Put your hands in your pockets. Leave the sugar there. Wipe off your thumb inside your pocket. Remember, you can use your friend's initial or a simple drawing instead of a triangle.

Dandelion Magic

Break a dandelion and make it whole again!

Your magician's tools: two dandelions and a stick small enough to fit in your pocket.

1. Break off the stem of one of the dandelions just under the bud.

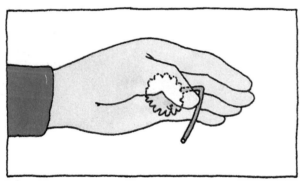

2. Hold the other dandelion in your hand. Bend the top part of the dandelion into your hand.

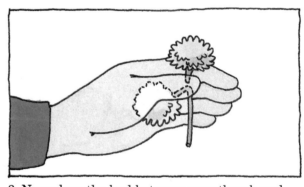

3. Now place the bud between your thumb and your fingers so it looks like it is coming from the stem. Put the stick near you.
Now your friend can come see your magic!

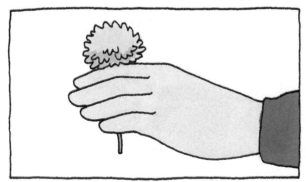

4. Show your friend the dandelion. Do not show him or her the inside of your hand.

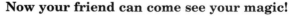
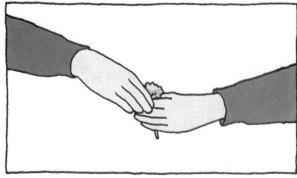

5. Grasp the bud with your other hand.

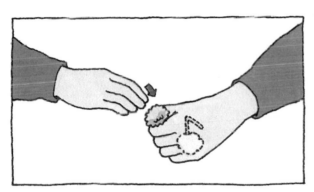

6. Pretend to break the bud off the stem. Show it to your friend.

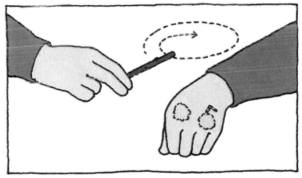

7. Close your hand in a fist around the whole dandelion.

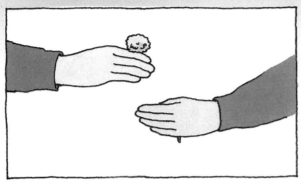

8. Put the bud into your fist.

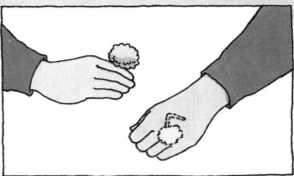

9. Pick up the stick, wave it like a magic wand over your fist, and say the magic words, "Flower, feel. Flower, heal." Set the stick down on the ground.

10. Reach into your fist and pull out the whole dandelion. Straighten it out. Give the dandelion to your friend. The bud is still in your fist.

11. Pick up the stick using the hand that still has the bud inside. Put the stick and the bud into your pocket.

Shadow Power

Make your shadow appear in a drawing!

Your magician's tools: a manila envelope, cardboard (smaller than the manila envelope), two small envelopes, two pieces of paper, double-sided tape, a paper cup, and a pencil.

1. Put two strips of double-sided tape on the front of each small envelope.

2. Stick one envelope onto the center of the piece of cardboard. Turn the cardboard over and stick the other envelope onto the center of this side.

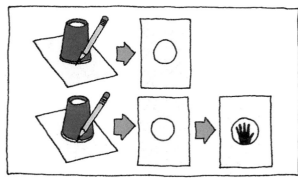

3. Put the cup on the center of one of the sheets of paper. Trace around the cup. Do the same to the second sheet of paper. On this sheet, draw a small black hand inside the circle.

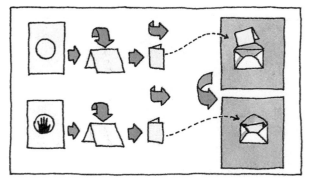

4. Fold each sheet of paper and place each in one of the small envelopes. Close the envelopes, but do not seal them.

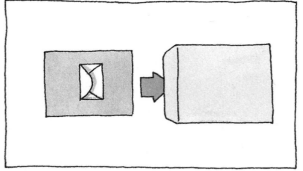

5. Place the cardboard in the manila envelope. Make sure the drawing with the hand is facing the front of the envelope.
Now your friend can come see your magic!

6. With the front of the manila envelope against your body, pull out the cardboard. Don't let your friend see the other side. Let her look inside the manila envelope to see it is empty.

7. Pull out the sheet of paper and have your friend unfold it. Say to her, "That circle is the sun." Then, have your friend fold the paper.

8. Put the folded paper back in the small envelope. Put the cardboard in the manila envelope again, with the side that has the drawing of the hand facing the front of the envelope.

9. Place the manila envelope on the ground. Hold your hand so the shadow of your hand is on the manila envelope. (This magic is best done on sunny days.)

10. Pick up the manila envelope and hold it with the back against your body. Take out the cardboard. Remove the paper from the small envelope.

11. Have your friend open it. The shadow of your hand is now in the sun! Put the paper and cardboard into the manila envelope, and place them in your backpack.

The Path of Magic

Long ago, most people believed in real magic. They believed in the magic they saw every day—magical things like the bright sun that rose every morning, the invisible wind, the colorful rainbow, and the shining moon in the dark night sky.

As time went by, people began to have fun performing different kinds of shows. One kind of show was the magic show.

Most magicians created their magic shows in the street. Some sat on the ground and some used a table they carried with them. The most famous trick of these street magicians was the cups and balls, in which three small balls appeared and vanished under three cups.

The Conjurer by Hieronymus Bosch/Musée Municipal, St. Germain-en-Laye

Some Famous Magicians

THE GRANGER COLLECTION, New York

At a fair in 1726, Issac Fawkes showed an empty bag; then he pulled out 100 eggs, handfuls of gold and silver coins, and several birds!

From the Todd Karr Collection

Later, magicians began doing magic shows in theaters. Robert-Houdin (1802–1871), a French magician, had a great magic show in which he floated his son in the air. He made him disappear, too!

THE GRANGER COLLECTION, New York

The most famous magician ever was Harry Houdini (1874–1926). He could escape from anything people locked him into!

Photo by Irving Desfor / Property of Vito Lupo

Slydini (1901–1992) was a great magician who was a master at fooling people while sitting just a few inches away from them.

NBC/GLOBE PHOTOS

Doug Henning (born 1947) has made a tiger appear, an elephant disappear, and walked through a brick wall in his wondrous magic shows in theaters and on television.

Sandoz Studios

Eugene Burger (born 1939) is a modern wizard who tells beautiful stories as he creates his illusions.

Photo by Eric Farber

Jeff McBride (born 1959) dances as he does his powerful magic with masks, music, and mime.